W9-BJU-951

THE TINKER'S WEDDING

HE TINKER'S WEDDING

A COMEDY IN TWO ACTS

By J. M. SYNGE

JOHN W. LUCE AND COMPANY
BOSTON : : : : : : : : : 1911

1911

PREFACE.

The drama is made serious — in the French sense of the word — not by the degree in which it is taken up with problems that are serious in themselves, but by the degree in which it gives the nourishment, not very easy to define, on which our imaginations live. We should not go to the theatre as we go to a chemist's, or a dram-shop, but as we go to a dinner, where the food we need is taken with pleasure and excitement. This was nearly always so in Spain and England and France when the drama was at its richest — the infancy and decay of the drama tend to be didactic — but in these days the playhouse is too often stocked with the drugs of many seedy problems, or with the absinthe or vermouth of the last musical comedy.

The drama, like the symphony, does not teach or prove anything. Analysts with their problems, and teachers with their systems, are soon as old-fashioned as the pharmacopœia of Galen,—look at Ibsen and the Germans — but the best plays of Ben Jonson and Molière can no more go out of fashion than the blackberries on the hedges.

Of the things which nourish the imagination humour is one of the most needful, and it is dangerous to limit or destroy it. Baudelaire calls laughter the greatest sign of the Satanic element in man; and where a country loses its humor, as some towns in Ireland are doing, there will be morbidity of mind, as Baudelaire's mind was morbid.

In the greater part of Ireland, however, the whole people, from the tinkers to the clergy, have still a life, and view of life, that are rich and genial and humorous. I do not think that these country people, who have so much humor themselves, will mind being laughed at without malice, as the people in every country have been laughed at in their own comedies.

J. M. S.

December 2nd, 1907.

THE TINKER'S WEDDING

PERSONS

MICHAEL BYRNE, a tinker.

MARY BYRNE, an old woman, his mother.

SARAH CASEY, a young tinker woman.

A PRIEST.

THE TINKER'S WEDDING

ACT I.

SCENE: *A Village roadside after nightfall. A fire of sticks is burning near the ditch a little to the right. Michael is working beside it. In the background, on the left, a sort of tent and ragged clothes drying on the hedge. On the right a chapel-gate.*

SARAH CASEY — *coming in on right, eagerly.*— We'll see his reverence this place, Michael Byrne, and he passing backward to his house to-night.

MICHAEL — *grimly.*— That'll be a sacred and a sainted joy!

SARAH — *sharply.*— It'll be small joy for yourself if you aren't ready with my wedding ring. (*She goes over to him.*) Is it near done this time, or what way is it at all?

MICHAEL. A poor way only, Sarah Casey, for it's the divil's job making a ring, and you'll be having my hands destroyed in a short while the way I'll not be able to make a tin can at all maybe at the dawn of day.

SARAH — *sitting down beside him and throwing sticks on the fire.*— If it's the divil's job, let you mind it, and leave your speeches that would choke a fool.

MICHAEL — *slowly and glumly.*— And it's you'll go talking of fools, Sarah Casey, when no man did ever hear a lying story even of your like unto this mortal day. You to be going beside me a great while, and rearing a lot of them, and then to be setting off with your talk of getting married, and your driving me to it, and I not asking it at all.

[*Sarah turns her back to him and arranges something in the ditch.*

MICHAEL — *angrily.*— Can't you speak a word when I'm asking what is it ails you since the moon did change?

SARAH — *musingly.*— I'm thinking there isn't anything ails me, Michael Byrne; but the spring-time is a queer time, and its queer thoughts maybe I do think at whiles.

MICHAEL. It's hard set you'd be to think queerer than welcome, Sarah Casey; but what will you gain dragging me to the priest this night, I'm saying, when it's new thoughts you'll be thinking at the dawn of day?

SARAH — *teasingly.*— It's at the dawn of day I do be thinking I'd have a right to be going off to the rich tinker's do be travelling from Tibradden to the Tara Hill; for it'd be a fine life to be driving with young Jaunting

Jim, where there wouldn't be any big hills to break the back of you, with walking up and walking down.

MICHAEL — *with dismay.*— It's the like of that you do be thinking!

SARAH. The like of that, Michael Byrne, when there is a bit of sun in it, and a kind air, and a great smell coming from the thorn trees is above your head.

MICHAEL — *looks at her for a moment with horror, and then hands her the ring.*— Will that fit you now?

SARAH — *trying it on.*— It's making it tight you are, and the edges sharp on the tin.

MICHAEL — *looking at it carefully.*— It's the fat of your own finger, Sarah Casey; and isn't it a mad thing I'm saying again that you'd be asking marriage of me, or making a talk of going away from me, and you thriving and getting your good health by the grace of the Almighty God?

SARAH — *giving it back to him.*— Fix it now, and it'll do, if you're wary you don't squeeze it again.

MICHAEL — *moodily, working again.*— It's easy saying be wary; there's many things easy said, Sarah Casey, you'd wonder a fool even would be saying at all. (*He starts vio-*

lently.) The divil mend you, I'm scalded again!

SARAH — *scornfully.*— If you are, it's a clumsy man you are this night, Michael Byrne (*raising her voice*); and let you make haste now, or herself will be coming with the porter.

MICHAEL — *defiantly, raising his voice.* Let me make haste? I'll be making haste maybe to hit you a great clout; for I'm thinking it's the like of that you want. I'm thinking on the day I got you above at Rathvanna, and the way you began crying out and we coming down off the hill, crying out and saying, "I'll go back to my ma," and I'm thinking on the way I came behind you that time, and hit you a great clout in the lug, and how quiet and easy it was you came along with me from that hour to this present day.

SARAH — *standing up and throwing all her sticks into the fire.*— And a big fool I was too, maybe; but we'll be seeing Jaunting Jim to-morrow in Ballinaclash, and he after getting a great price for his white foal in the horse-fair of Wicklow, the way it'll be a great sight to see him squandering his share of gold, and he with a grand eye for a fine horse, and a grand eye for a woman.

MICHAEL — *working again with impa-*

tience.— The divil do him good with the two of them.

SARAH — *kicking up the ashes with her foot.*— Ah, he's a great lad, I'm telling you, and it's proud and happy I'll be to see him, and he the first one called me the Beauty of Ballinacree, a fine name for a woman.

MICHAEL — *with contempt.*— It's the like of that name they do be putting on the horses they have below racing in Arklow. It's easy pleased you are, Sarah Casey, easy pleased with a big word, or the liar speaks it.

SARAH. Liar!

MICHAEL. Liar, surely.

SARAH — *indignantly.*— Liar, is it? Didn't you ever hear tell of the peelers followed me ten miles along the Glen Malure, and they talking love to me in the dark night, or of the children you'll meet coming from school and they saying one to the other, "It's this day we seen Sarah Casey, the Beauty of Ballinacree, a great sight surely."

MICHAEL. God help the lot of them!

SARAH. It's yourself you'll be calling God to help, in two weeks or three, when you'll be waking up in the dark night and thinking you see me coming with the sun on me, and I driving a high cart with Jaunting

Jim going behind. It's lonesome and cold you'll be feeling the ditch where you'll be lying down that night, I'm telling you, and you hearing the old woman making a great noise in her sleep, and the bats squeaking in the trees.

MICHAEL. Whist. I hear some one coming the road.

SARAH — *looking out right.*— It's some one coming forward from the doctor's door.

MICHAEL. It's often his reverence does be in there playing cards, or drinking a sup, or singing songs, until the dawn of day.

SARAH. It's a big boast of a man with a long step on him and a trumpeting voice. It's his reverence surely; and if you have the ring done, it's a great bargain we'll make now and he after drinking his glass.

MICHAEL — *going to her and giving her the ring.*— There's your ring, Sarah Casey; but I'm thinking he'll walk by and not stop to speak with the like of us at all.

SARAH — *tidying herself, in great excitement.*— Let you be sitting here and keeping a great blaze, the way he can look on my face; and let you seem to be working, for it's great love the like of him have to talk of work.

MICHAEL — *moodily, sitting down and*

beginning to work at a tin can.— Great love surely.

SARAH — *eagerly.*—Make a great blaze now, Michael Byrne.

[*The priest comes in on right; she comes forward in front of him.*

SARAH — *in a very plausible voice.*— Good evening, your reverence. It's a grand fine night, by the grace of God.

PRIEST. The Lord have mercy on us! What kind of a living woman is it that you are at all?

SARAH. It's Sarah Casey I am, your reverence, the Beauty of Ballinacree, and it's Michael Byrne is below in the ditch.

PRIEST. A holy pair, surely! Let you get out of my way. [*He tries to pass by.*

SARAH — *keeping in front of him.*— We are wanting a little word with your reverence.

PRIEST. I haven't a halfpenny at all. Leave the road I'm saying.

SARAH. It isn't a halfpenny we're asking, holy father; but we were thinking maybe we'd have a right to be getting married; and we were thinking it's yourself would marry us for not a halfpenny at all; for you're a kind man, your reverence, a kind man with the poor.

PRIEST — *with astonishment.*— Is it marry you for nothing at all?

SARAH. It is, your reverence; and we were thinking maybe you'd give us a little small bit of silver to pay for the ring.

PRIEST — *loudly.*— Let you hold your tongue; let you be quiet, Sarah Casey. I've no silver at all for the like of you; and if you want to be married, let you pay your pound. I'd do it for a pound only, and that's making it a sight cheaper than I'd make it for one of my own pairs is living here in the place.

SARAH. Where would the like of us get a pound, your reverence?

PRIEST. Wouldn't you easy get it with your selling asses, and making cans, and your stealing east and west in Wicklow and Wexford and the county Meath? (*He tries to pass her.*) Let you leave the road, and not be plaguing me more.

SARAH — *pleadingly, taking money from her pocket.*— Wouldn't you have a little mercy on us, your reverence? (*Holding out money.*) Wouldn't you marry us for a half a sovereign, and it a nice shiny one with a view on it of the living king's mamma?

PRIEST. If it's ten shillings you have, let you get ten more the same way, and I'll marry you then.

SARAH — *whining.*— It's two years we are getting that bit, your reverence, with our pence and our halfpence and an odd threepenny bit; and if you don't marry us now, himself and the old woman, who has a great drouth, will be drinking it to-morrow in the fair (*she puts her apron to her eyes, half sobbing*), and then I won't be married any time, and I'll be saying till I'm an old woman: "It's a cruel and a wicked thing to be bred poor."

PRIEST — *turning up towards the fire.*— Let you not be crying, Sarah Casey. It's a queer woman you are to be crying at the like of that, and you your whole life walking the roads.

SARAH — *sobbing.*— It's two years we are getting the gold, your reverence, and now you won't marry us for that bit, and we hard-working poor people do be making cans in the dark night, and blinding our eyes with the black smoke from the bits of twigs we do be burning.

[*An old woman is heard singing tipsily on the left.*

PRIEST — *looking at the can Michael is making.*— When will you have that can done, Michael Byrne?

MICHAEL. In a short space only, your

reverence, for I'm putting the last dab of solder on the rim.

PRIEST. Let you get a crown along with the ten shillings and the gallon can, Sarah Casey, and I will wed you so.

MARY — *suddenly shouting behind, tipsily.*— Larry was a fine lad, I'm saying; Larry was a fine lad, Sarah Casey ——

MICHAEL. Whist, now, the two of you. There's my mother coming, and she'd have us destroyed if she heard the like of that talk the time she's been drinking her fill.

MARY — *comes in singing* —

And when we asked him what way he'd die,
  And he hanging unrepented,
" Begob," says Larry, " that's all in my eye,
  By the clergy first invented."

SARAH. Give me the jug now, or you'll have it spilt in the ditch.

MARY — *holding the jug with both her hands, in a stilted voice.*— Let you leave me easy, Sarah Casey. I won't spill it, I'm saying. God help you; are you thinking it's frothing full to the brim it is at this hour of the night, and I after carrying it in my two hands a long step from Jemmy Neill's?

MICHAEL — *anxiously.*— Is there a sup left at all?

SARAH — *looking into the jug.*— A little small sup only I'm thinking.

MARY — *sees the priest, and holds out jug towards him.*— God save your reverence. I'm after bringing down a smart drop; and let you drink it up now, for it's a middling drouthy man you are at all times, God forgive you, and this night is cruel dry.

[*She tries to go towards him. Sarah holds her back.*

PRIEST — *waving her away.*— Let you not be falling to the flames. Keep off, I'm saying.

MARY — *persuasively.*— Let you not be shy of us, your reverence. Aren't we all sinners, God help us! Drink a sup now, I'm telling you; and we won't let on a word about it till the Judgment Day.

[*She takes up a tin mug, pours some porter into it, and gives it to him.*

MARY — *singing, and holding the jug in her hand* —

A lonesome ditch in Ballygan
The day you're beating a tenpenny can;
A lonesome bank in Ballyduff
The time . . . [*She breaks off.*

It's a bad, wicked song, Sarah Casey; and let you put me down now in the ditch, and I won't sing it till himself will be gone; for it's bad enough he is, I'm thinking, without ourselves making him worse.

SARAH — *putting her down, to the priest, half laughing.*— Don't mind her at all, your reverence. She's no shame the time she's a drop taken; and if it was the Holy Father from Rome was in it, she'd give him a little sup out of her mug, and say the same as she'd say to yourself.

MARY — *to the priest.*— Let you drink it up, holy father. Let you drink it up, I'm saying, and not be letting on you wouldn't do the like of it, and you with a stack of pint bottles above, reaching the sky.

PRIEST — *with resignation.*— Well, here's to your good health, and God forgive us all.

[*He drinks.*

MARY. That's right now, your reverence, and the blessing of God be on you. Isn't it a grand thing to see you sitting down, with no pride in you, and drinking a sup with the like of us, and we the poorest, wretched, starving creatures you'd see any place on the earth?

PRIEST. If it's starving you are itself, I'm thinking it's well for the like of you that do be drinking when there's drouth on you, and lying down to sleep when your legs are stiff. (*He sighs gloomily.*) What would you do if it was the like of myself you were, saying Mass with your mouth dry, and running east and west for a sick call maybe, and hearing the rural people again and they saying their sins?

MARY — *with compassion.*— It's destroyed you must be hearing the sins of the rural people on a fine spring.

PRIEST — *with despondency.*— It's a hard life, I'm telling you, a hard life, Mary Byrne; and there's the bishop coming in the morning, and he an old man, would have you destroyed if he seen a thing at all.

MARY — *with great sympathy.* — It'd break my heart to hear you talking and sighing the like of that, your reverence. (*She pats him on the knee.*) Let you rouse up, now, if it's a poor, single man you are itself, and I'll be singing you songs unto the dawn of day.

PRIEST — *interrupting her.*— What is it I want with your songs when it'd be better for the like of you, that'll soon die, to be down on your two knees saying prayers to the Almighty God?

MARY. If it's prayers I want, you'd have a right to say one yourself, holy father; for we don't have them at all, and I've heard tell a power of times it's that you're for. Say one now, your reverence, for I've heard a power of queer things and I walking the world, but there's one thing I never heard any time, and that's a real priest saying a prayer.

PRIEST. The Lord protect us!

MARY. It's no lie, holy father. I often heard the rural people making a queer noise and they going to rest; but who'd mind the like of them? And I'm thinking it should be great game to hear a scholar, the like of you, speaking Latin to the saints above.

PRIEST — *scandalized.*— Stop your talking, Mary Byrne; you're an old flagrant heathen, and I'll stay no more with the lot of you. [*He rises.*

MARY — *catching hold of him.*— Stop till you say a prayer, your reverence; stop till you say a little prayer, I'm telling you, and I'll give you my blessing and the last sup from the jug.

PRIEST — *breaking away.*— Leave me go, Mary Byrne; for I have never met your like for hard abominations the score and two years I'm living in the place.

MARY — *innocently.*—Is that the truth?

PRIEST.— It is, then, and God have mercy on your soul.

[*The priest goes towards the left, and Sarah follows him.*

SARAH — *in a low voice.*— And what time will you do the thing I'm asking, holy father? for I'm thinking you'll do it surely, and not have me growing into an old, wicked heathen like herself.

MARY — *calling out shrilly.*— Let you be walking back here, Sarah Casey, and not be talking whisper-talk with the like of him in the face of the Almighty God.

SARAH — *to the priest.*— Do you hear her now, your reverence? Isn't it true, surely, she's an old, flagrant heathen, would destroy the world?

PRIEST — *to Sarah, moving off.*— Well, I'll be coming down early to the chapel, and let you come to me a while after you see me passing, and bring the bit of gold along with you, and the tin can. I'll marry you for them two, though it's a pitiful small sum; for I wouldn't be easy in my soul if I left you growing into an old, wicked heathen the like of her.

SARAH — *following him out.*— The blessing of the Almighty God be on you, holy father, and that He may reward and watch you from this present day.

MARY — *nudging Michael.*— Did you see that, Michael Byrne? Didn't you hear me telling you she's flighty a while back since the change of the moon? With her fussing for marriage, and she making whisper-talk with one man or another man along by the road.

MICHAEL.— Whist now, or she'll knock the head of you the time she comes back.

MARY.— Ah, it's a bad, wicked way the world is this night, if there's a fine air in it itself. You'd never have seen me, and I a young woman, making whisper-talk with the like of him, and he the fearfullest old fellow you'd see any place walking the world.

[*Sarah comes back quickly.*

MARY — *calling out to her.*— What is it you're after whispering above with himself?

SARAH — *exultingly.*— Lie down, and leave us in peace. *She whispers with Michael.*

MARY — *poking out her pipe with a straw, sings* —

She'd whisper with one, and she'd whisper
with two——

She breaks off coughing.— My singing voice is gone for this night, Sarah Casey. (*She lights her pipe.*) But if it's flighty you are itself, you're a grand handsome woman, the glory of tinkers, the pride of Wicklow, the Beauty of Ballinacree. I wouldn't have you lying down and you lonesome to sleep this night in a dark ditch when the spring is coming in the trees; so let you sit down there by the big bough, and I'll be telling you the finest story you'd hear any place from Dundalk to Ballinacree, with great queens in it, making themselves matches from the start to the end, and they with shiny silks on them the length of the day, and white shifts for the night.

MICHAEL — *standing up with the tin can in his hand.*— Let you go asleep, and not have us destroyed.

MARY — *lying back sleepily.*— Don't mind him, Sarah Casey. Sit down now, and I'll be telling you a story would be fit to tell a woman the like of you in the springtime of the year.

SARAH — *taking the can from Michael, and tying it up in a piece of sacking.*— That'll not be rusting now in the dews of night. I'll put it up in the ditch the way it will be handy in the morning; and now we've that done, Michael Byrne, I'll go along with you and welcome for Tim Flaherty's hens.

[*She puts the can in the ditch.*

MARY — *sleepily.*— I've a grand story of the great queens of Ireland with white necks on them the like of Sarah Casey, and fine arms would hit you a slap the way Sarah Casey would hit you.

SARAH — *beckoning on the left.*— Come along now, Michael, while she's falling asleep.

[*He goes towards left. Mary sees that they are going, starts up suddenly, and turns over on her hands and knees.*

MARY — *piteously.*— Where is it you're going? Let you walk back here, and not be leaving me lonesome when the night is fine.

SARAH. Don't be waking the world with your talk when we're going up through the back wood to get two of Tim Flaherty's hens are roosting in the ash-tree above at the well.

MARY. And it's leaving me lone you are? Come back here, Sarah Casey. Come back here, I'm saying; or if it's off you must go, leave me the two little coppers you have, the way I can walk up in a short while, and get another pint for my sleep.

SARAH. It's too much you have taken. Let you stretch yourself out and take a long sleep; for isn't that the best thing any woman can do, and she an old drinking heathen like yourself.

[*She and Michael go out left.*

MARY — *standing up slowly.*— It's gone they are, and I with my feet that weak under me you'd knock me down with a rush, and my head with a noise in it the like of what you'd hear in a stream and it running between two rocks and rain falling. (*She goes over to the ditch where the can is tied in sacking, and takes it down.*) What good am I this night, God help me? What good are the grand stories I have when it's few would listen to an old woman, few but a girl maybe would be in great fear the time her hour was come, or a little child wouldn't be sleeping with the hunger on a cold night? (*She takes the can from the sacking and fits in three empty bottles and straw in its place, and ties them up.*) Maybe the two of them have a good right to be walking out the little short while they'd be young; but if they have itself, they'll not keep Mary Byrne from her full pint when the night's fine, and there's a dry moon in the sky. (*She takes up the can, and puts the package back in the ditch.*) Jemmy Neill's a decent lad; and he'll give me a good drop for the can; and maybe if I keep near the peelers to-morrow for the first bit of the fair, herself won't strike me at all; and if she does itself, what's a little stroke on your head beside sitting lonesome on a fine night, hearing the dogs barking, and the bats squeaking, and you saying over, it's a short while only till you die.

[*She goes out singing " The night before Larry was stretched."*

CURTAIN

ACT II.

SCENE: *The same. Early morning. Sarah is washing her face in an old bucket; then plaits her hair. Michael is tidying himself also. Mary Byrne is asleep against the ditch.*

SARAH — *to Michael, with pleased excitement.*—Go over, now, to the bundle beyond, and you'll find a kind of a red handkerchief to put upon your neck, and a green one for myself.

MICHAEL — *getting them.*— You're after spending more money on the like of them. Well, it's a power we're losing this time, and we not gaining a thing at all. (*With the handkerchief.*) Is it them two?

SARAH. It is, Michael. (*She takes one of them.*) Let you tackle that one round under your chin; and let you not forget to take your hat from your head when we go up into the church. I asked Biddy Flynn below, that's after marrying her second man, and she told me it's the like of that they do.

[*Mary yawns, and turns over in her sleep.*

SARAH — *with anxiety.*— There she is waking up on us, and I thinking we'd have the job done before she'd know of it at all.

MICHAEL. She'll be crying out now, and making game of us, and saying it's fools we are surely.

SARAH. I'll send her to sleep again, or get her out of it one way or another; for it'd be a bad case to have a divil's scholar the like of her turning the priest against us maybe with her godless talk.

MARY — *waking up, and looking at them with curiosity, blandly.*— That's fine things you have on you, Sarah Casey; and it's a great stir you're making this day, washing your face. I'm that used to the hammer, I wouldn't hear it at all, but washing is a rare thing, and you're after waking me up, and I having a great sleep in the sun.

[*She looks around cautiously at the bundle in which she has hidden the bottles.*

SARAH — *coaxingly.*— Let you stretch out again for a sleep, Mary Byrne, for it'll be a middling time yet before we go to the fair.

MARY — *with suspicion.*— That's a sweet tongue you have, Sarah Casey; but if sleep's a grand thing, it's a grand thing to be waking up a day the like of this, when there's a warm sun in it, and a kind air, and you'll hear the cuckoos singing and crying out on the top of the hills.

SARAH. If it's that gay you are, you'd have a right to walk down and see would you get a few halfpence from the rich men do be driving early to the fair.

MARY. When rich men do be driving early, it's queer tempers they have, the Lord forgive them; the way it's little but bad words and swearing out you'd get from them all.

SARAH — *losing her temper and breaking out fiercely.*— Then if you'll neither beg nor sleep, let you walk off from this place where you're not wanted, and not have us waiting for you maybe at the turn of day.

MARY — *rather uneasy, turning to Michael.*— God help our spirits, Michael; there she is again rousing cranky from the break of dawn. Oh! isn't she a terror since the moon did change (*she gets up slowly*)? And I'd best be going forward to sell the gallon can.

[*She goes over and takes up the bundle.*

SARAH — *crying out angrily.*— Leave that down, Mary Byrne. Oh! aren't you the scorn of women to think that you'd have that drouth and roguery on you that you'd go drinking the can and the dew not dried from the grass?

MARY — *in a feigned tone of pacification, with the bundle still in her hand.*— It's not a drouth but a heartburn I have this day, Sarah Casey, so I'm going down to cool my gullet at the blessed well; and I'll sell the can to the parson's daughter below, a harmless poor creature would fill your hand with shillings for a brace of lies.

SARAH. Leave down the tin can, Mary Byrne, for I hear the drouth upon your tongue to-day.

MARY. There's not a drink-house from this place to the fair, Sarah Casey; the way you'll find me below with the full price, and not a farthing gone.

[*She turns to go off left.*

SARAH — *jumping up, and picking up the hammer threateningly.*— Put down that can, I'm saying.

MARY — *looking at her for a moment in terror, and putting down the bundle in the ditch.*— Is it raving mad you're going, Sarah Casey, and you the pride of women to destroy the world?

SARAH — *going up to her, and giving her a push off left.*— I'll show you if it's raving mad I am. Go on from this place, I'm saying, and be wary now.

MARY — *turning back after her.*— If I

go, I'll be telling old and young you're a weathered heathen savage, Sarah Casey, the one did put down a head of the parson's cabbage to boil in the pot with your clothes (*the priest comes in behind her, on the left, and listens*), and quenched the flaming candles on the throne of God the time your shadow fell within the pillars of the chapel door.

[*Sarah turns on her, and she springs round nearly into the Priest's arms. When she sees him, she claps her shawl over her mouth, and goes up towards the ditch, laughing to herself.*

PRIEST — *going to Sarah, half terrified at the language that he has heard.*— Well, aren't you a fearful lot? I'm thinking it's only humbug you were making at the fall of night, and you won't need me at all.

SARAH — *with anger still in her voice.*— Humbug is it! would you be turning back upon your spoken promise in the face of God?

PRIEST — *dubiously.*— I'm thinking you were never christened, Sarah Casey; and it would be a queer job to go dealing Christian sacraments unto the like of you. (*Persuasively feeling in his pocket.*) So it would be best, maybe, I'd give you a shilling for to drink my health, and let you walk on, and not trouble me at all.

SARAH. That's your talking, is it? If you don't stand to your spoken word, holy father, I'll make my own complaint to the mitred bishop in the face of all.

PRIEST. You'd do that!

SARAH. I would surely, holy father, if I walked to the city of Dublin with blood and blisters on my naked feet.

PRIEST — *uneasily scratching his ear.*— I wish this day was done, Sarah Casey; for I'm thinking it's a risky thing getting mixed up in any matters with the like of you.

SARAH. Be hast-- then, and you'll have us done with before you'd think at all.

PRIEST — *giving in.*— Well, maybe it's right you are, and let you come up to the chapel when you see me looking from the door.

[*He goes up into the chapel.*

SARAH — *calling after him.*— We will, and God preserve you, holy father.

MARY — *coming down to them, speaking with amazement and consternation, but without anger.*— Going to the chapel! It's at marriage you're fooling again, maybe? (*Sarah turns her back on her.*) It was for that you were washing your face, and you after sending me for porter at the fall of night the way I'd drink a good half from the jug? (*Going *round in front of Sarah.*) Is it at marriage you're fooling again?

SARAH — *triumphantly.*— It is, Mary Byrne. I'll be married now in a short while; and from this day there will no one have a right to call me a dirty name and I selling cans in Wicklow or Wexford or the city of Dublin itself.

MARY — *turning to Michael.*— And it's yourself is wedding her, Michael Byrne?

MICHAEL — *gloomily.*— It is, God spare us.

MARY — *looks at Sarah for a moment, and then bursts out into a laugh of derision.*— Well, she's a tight, hardy girl, and it's no lie; but I never knew till this day it was a black born fool I had for a son. You'll breed asses, I've heard them say, and poaching dogs, and horses'd go licking the wind, but it's a hard thing, God help me, to breed sense in a son.

MICHAEL — *gloomily.*— If I didn't marry her, she'd be walking off to Jaunting Jim maybe at the fall of night; and it's well yourself knows there isn't the like of her for getting money and selling songs to the men.

MARY. And you're thinking it's paying gold to his reverence would make a woman stop when she's a mind to go?

SARAH — *angrily.*— Let you not be destroying us with your talk when I've as good a right to a decent marriage as any speckled female does be sleeping in the black hovels above, would choke a mule.

MARY — *soothingly.*— It's as good a right you have surely, Sarah Casey, but what good will it do? Is it putting that ring on your finger will keep you from getting an aged woman and losing the fine face you have, or be easing your pains, when it's the grand ladies do be married in silk dresses, with rings of gold, that do pass any woman with their share of torment in the hour of birth, and do be paying the doctors in the city of Dublin a great price at that time, the like of what you'd pay for a good ass and a cart?

[*She sits down.*

SARAH — *puzzled.*— Is that the truth?

MARY — *pleased with the point she has made.*— Wouldn't any know it's the truth? Ah, it's a few short years you are yet in the world, Sarah Casey, and it's little or nothing at all maybe you know about it.

SARAH — *vehement but uneasy.*— What is it yourself knows of the fine ladies when they wouldn't let the like of you go near them at all?

MARY. If you do be drinking a little sup in one town and another town, it's soon you get great knowledge and a great sight into the world. You'll see men there, and women there, sitting up on the ends of barrels in the dark night, and they making great talk would soon have the like of you, Sarah Casey, as wise as a March hare.

MICHAEL — *to Sarah.*— That's the truth she's saying, and maybe if you've sense in you at all, you'd have a right still to leave your fooling, and not be wasting our gold.

SARAH — *decisively.*— If it's wise or fool I am, I've made a good bargain and I'll stand to it now.

MARY. What is it he's making you give?

MICHAEL. The ten shillings in gold, and the tin can is above tied in the sack.

MARY — *looking at the bundle with surprise and dread.*— The bit of gold and the tin can, is it?

MICHAEL. The half a sovereign, and the gallon can.

MARY — *scrambling to her feet quickly.*— Well, I think I'll be walking off the road to the fair the way you won't be destroying me going too fast on the hills. (*She goes a few steps towards the left, then turns and speaks to Sarah very persuasively.*— Let you not take the can from the sack, Sarah Casey; for the people is coming above would be making game of you, and pointing their fingers if they seen you do the like of that. Let you leave it safe in the bag, I'm saying, Sarah darling. It's that way will be best.

[*She goes towards left, and pauses for a moment, looking about her with embarrassment.*

MICHAEL — *in a low voice.*— What ails her at all?

SARAH — *anxiously.*— It's real wicked she does be when you hear her speaking as easy as that.

MARY — *to herself.*— I'd be safer in the chapel, I'm thinking; for if she caught me after on the road, maybe she would kill me then.

[*She comes hobbling back towards the right.*

SARAH. Where is it you're going? It isn't that way we'll be walking to the fair.

MARY. I'm going up into the chapel to give you my blessing and hear the priest saying his prayers. It's a lonesome road is running below to Greenane, and a woman would never know the things might happen her and she walking single in a lonesome place.

[*As she reaches the chapel-gate, the Priest comes to it in his surplice.*

PRIEST — *crying out.*— Come along now.

It is the whole day you'd keep me here saying my prayers, and I getting my death with not a bit in my stomach, and my breakfast in ruins, and the Lord Bishop maybe driving on the road to-day?

SARAH. We're coming now, holy father.

PRIEST. Give me the bit of gold into my hand.

SARAH. It's here, holy father.

[*She gives it to him. Michael takes the bundle from the ditch and brings it over, standing a little behind Sarah. He feels the bundle, and looks at Mary with a meaning look.*

PRIEST — *looking at the gold.*— It's a good one, I'm thinking, wherever you got it. And where is the can?

SARAH — *taking the bundle.*— We have it here in a bit of clean sack, your reverence. We tied it up in the inside of that to keep it from rusting in the dews of night, and let you not open it now or you'll have the people making game of us and telling the story on us, east and west to the butt of the hills.

PRIEST — *taking the bundle.* — Give it here into my hand, Sarah Casey. What is it any person would think of a tinker making a can. [*He begins opening the bundle.*

SARAH. It's a fine can, your reverence.

for if it's poor simple people we are, it's fine cans we can make, and himself, God help him, is a great man surely at the trade.

[*Priest opens the bundle; the three empty bottles fall out.*

SARAH. Glory to the saints of joy!

PRIEST. Did ever any man see the like of that? To think you'd be putting deceit on me, and telling lies to me, and I going to marry you for a little sum wouldn't marry a child.

SARAH — *crestfallen and astonished.*— It's the divil did it, your reverence, and I wouldn't tell you a lie. (*Raising her hands.*) May the Lord Almighty strike me dead if the divil isn't after hooshing the tin can from the bag.

PRIEST — *vehemently.*— Go along now, and don't be swearing your lies. Go along now, and let you not be thinking I'm big fool enough to believe the like of that, when it's after selling it you are or making a swap for drink of it, maybe, in the darkness of the night.

MARY — *in a peacemaking voice, putting her hand on the Priest's left arm.*— She wouldn't do the like of that, your reverence, when she hasn't a decent standing drouth on her at all; and she's setting great store on her marriage the way you'd have a right to be taking her easy, and not minding the can. What differ would an empty can make with a fine, rich, hardy man the like of you?

SARAH — *imploringly.*— Marry us, your reverence, for the ten shillings in gold, and we'll make you a grand can in the evening — a can would be fit to carry water for the holy man of God. Marry us now and I'll be saying fine prayers for you, morning and night, if it'd be raining itself, and it'd be in two black pools I'd be setting my knees.

PRIEST — *loudly.*— It's a wicked, thieving, lying, scheming lot you are, the pack of you. Let you walk off now and take every stinking rag you have there from the ditch.

MARY — *putting her shawl over her head.* Marry her, your reverence, for the love of God, for there'll be queer doings below if you send her off the like of that and she swearing crazy on the road.

SARAH — *angrily.*— It's the truth she's saying; for it's herself, I'm thinking, is after swapping the tin can for a pint, the time she was raging mad with the drouth, and ourselves above walking the hill.

MARY — *crying out with indignation.*— Have you no shame, Sarah Casey, to tell lies unto a holy man?

SARAH — *to Mary, working herself into*

a rage.— It's making game of me you'd be, and putting a fool's head on me in the face of the world; but if you were thinking to be mighty cute walking off, or going up to hide in the church, I've got you this time, and you'll not run from me now.

[*She seizes up one of the bottles.*

MARY — *hiding behind the priest.*— Keep her off, your reverence, keep her off for the love of the Almighty God. What at all would the Lord Bishop say if he found me here lying with my head broken across, or the two of yous maybe digging a bloody grave for me at the door of the church?

PRIEST — *waving Sarah off.*— Go along, Sarah Casey. Would you be doing murder at my feet? Go along from me now, and wasn't I a big fool to have to do with you when it's nothing but distraction and torment I get from the kindness of my heart?

SARAH — *shouting.*— I've bet a power of strong lads east and west through the world, and are you thinking I'd turn back from a priest? Leave the road now, or maybe I would strike yourself.

PRIEST. You would not, Sarah Casey. I've no fear for the lot of you; but let you walk off, I'm saying, and not be coming where you've no business, and screeching tumult and murder at the doorway of the church.

SARAH. I'll not go a step till I have her head broke, or till I'm wed with himself. If you want to get shut of us, let you marry us now, for I'm thinking the ten shillings in gold is a good price for the like of you, and you near burst with the fat.

PRIEST. I wouldn't have you coming in on me and soiling my church; for there's nothing at all, I'm thinking, would keep the like of you from hell. (*He throws down the ten shillings on the ground.*) Gather up your gold now, and begone from my sight, for if ever I set an eye on you again you'll hear me telling the peelers who it was stole the black ass belonging to Philly O'Cullen, and whose hay it is the grey ass does be eating.

SARAH. You'd do that?

PRIEST. I would, surely.

SARAH. If you do, you'll be getting all the tinkers from Wicklow and Wexford, and the County Meath, to put up block tin in the place of glass to shield your windows where you do be looking out and blinking at the girls. It's hard set you'll be that time, I'm telling you, to fill the depth of your belly the long days of Lent; for we wouldn't leave a laying pullet in your yard at all.

PRIEST — *losing his temper finally.*— Go on, now, or I'll send the Lords of Justice a dated story of your villainies — burning, stealing, robbing, raping to this mortal day. Go on now, I'm saying, if you'd run from Kilmainham or the rope itself.

MICHAEL — *taking off his coat.*— Is it run from the like of you, holy father? Go up to your own shanty, or I'll beat you with the ass's reins till the world would hear you roaring from this place to the coast of Clare.

PRIEST. Is it lift your hand upon myself when the Lord would blight your members if you'd touch me now? Go on from this.

[*He gives him a shove.*

MICHAEL. Blight me is it? Take it then, your reverence, and God help you so.

[*He runs at him with the reins.*

PRIEST — *runs up to ditch crying out.*— There are the peelers passing by the grace of God —— hey, below!

MARY — *clapping her hand over his mouth.*— Knock him down on the road; they didn't hear him at all.

[*Michael pulls him down.*

SARAH. Gag his jaws.

MARY. Stuff the sacking in his teeth.

[*They gag him with the sack that had the can in it.*

SARAH. Tie the bag around his head, and if the peelers come, we'll put him head-first in the boghole is beyond the ditch.

[*They tie him up in some sacking.*

MICHAEL — *to Mary.*— Keep him quiet, and the rags tight on him for fear he'd screech. (*He goes back to their camp.*) Hurry with the things, Sarah Casey. The peelers aren't coming this way, and maybe we'll get off from them now.

[*They bundle the things together in wild haste, the priest wriggling and struggling about on the ground, with old Mary trying to keep him quiet.*

MARY — *patting his head.*— Be quiet, your reverence. What is it ails you, with your wrigglings now? Is it choking maybe? (*She puts her hand under the sack, and feels his mouth, patting him on the back.*) It's only letting on you are, holy father, for your nose is blowing back and forward as easy as an east wind on an April day. (*In a soothing voice.*) There now, holy father, let you stay easy, I'm telling you, and learn a little sense and patience, the way you'll not be so airy again going to rob poor sinners of their scraps of gold. (*He gets quieter.*) That's a good boy you are now, your reverence, and let you not be uneasy, for we wouldn't hurt you at all. It's sick and sorry we are to tease you; but what did you want meddling with the like of us, when it's a long time we are going our own ways — father and son, and his son after him, or mother and daughter, and her own daughter again — and it's little need we ever had of going up into a church and swearing — I'm told there's swearing with it — a word no man would believe, or with drawing rings on our fingers, would be cutting our skins maybe when we'd be taking the ass from the shafts, and pulling the straps the time they'd be slippy with going around beneath the heavens in rains falling.

MICHAEL — *who has finished bundling up the things, comes over to Sarah.*— We're fixed now; and I have a mind to run him in a boghole the way he'll not be tattling to the peelers of our games to-day.

SARAH. You'd have a right too, I'm thinking.

MARY — *soothingly.*— Let you not be rough with him, Sarah Casey, and he after drinking his sup of porter with us at the fall of night. Maybe he'd swear a mighty oath he wouldn't harm us, and then we'd safer loose him; for if we went to drown him, they'd maybe hang the batch of us, man and child and woman, and the ass itself.

MICHAEL. What would he care for an oath?

MARY. Don't you know his like do live in terror of the wrath of God? (*Putting her mouth to the Priest's ear in the sacking.*) Would you swear an oath, holy father, to leave us in our freedom, and not talk at all? (*Priest nods in sacking.*) Didn't I tell you? Look at the poor fellow nodding his head off in the bias of the sacks. Strip them off from him, and he'll be easy now.

MICHAEL — *as if speaking to a horse.*— Hold up, holy father.

[*He pulls the sacking off, and shows the priest with his hair on end. They free his mouth.*

MARY. Hold him till he swears.

PRIEST — *in a faint voice.*— I swear surely. If you let me go in peace, I'll not inform against you or say a thing at all, and may God forgive me for giving heed unto your like to-day.

SARAH — *puts the ring on his finger.*— There's the ring, holy father, to keep you minding of your oath until the end of time; for my heart's scalded with your fooling; and it'll be a long day till I go making talk of marriage or the like of that.

MARY — *complacently, standing up slow-*

ly.— She's vexed now, your reverence; and let you not mind her at all, for she's right surely, and it's little need we ever had of the like of you to get us our bit to eat, and our bit to drink, and our time of love when we were young men and women, and were fine to look at.

MICHAEL. Hurry on now. He's a great man to have kept us from fooling our gold; and we'll have a great time drinking that bit with the trampers on the green of Clash.

[*They gather up their things. The priest stands up.*

PRIEST — *lifting up his hand.*— I've sworn not to call the hand of man upon your crimes to-day; but I haven't sworn I wouldn't call the fire of heaven from the hand of the Almighty God.

[*He begins saying a Latin malediction in a loud ecclesiastical voice.*

MARY. There's an old villain.

ALL — *together.*— Run, run. Run for your lives.

[*They rush out, leaving the Priest master of the situation.*

CURTAIN